CAR & TRUCK

PRESCHOOL

MATH

WORKBOOK for TODDLERS

MORE KIDS' ACTIVITY BOOKS FROM US
https://k-imagine-pub.com/

1  **one**

2 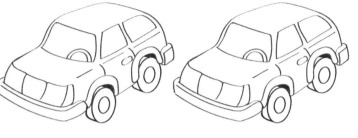 **two**

3  **three**

4  **four**

5 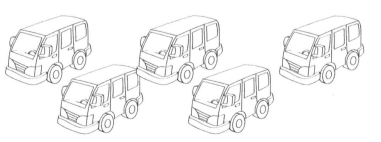 **five**

6 six

7 seven

8 eight

9 nine

10 ten

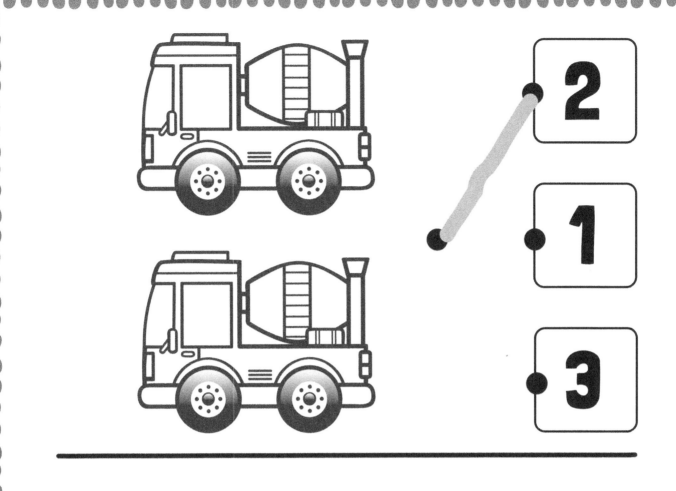

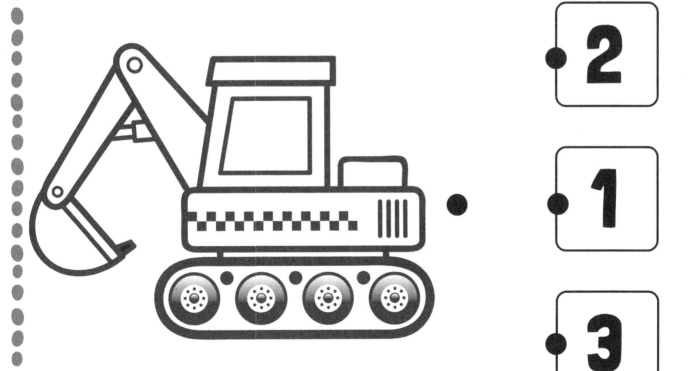

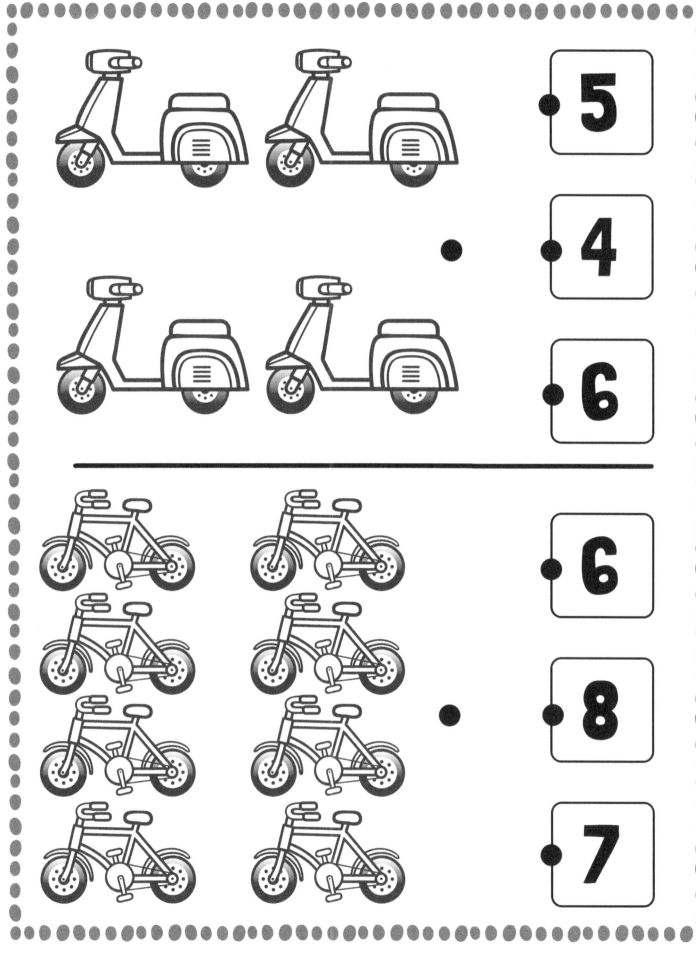

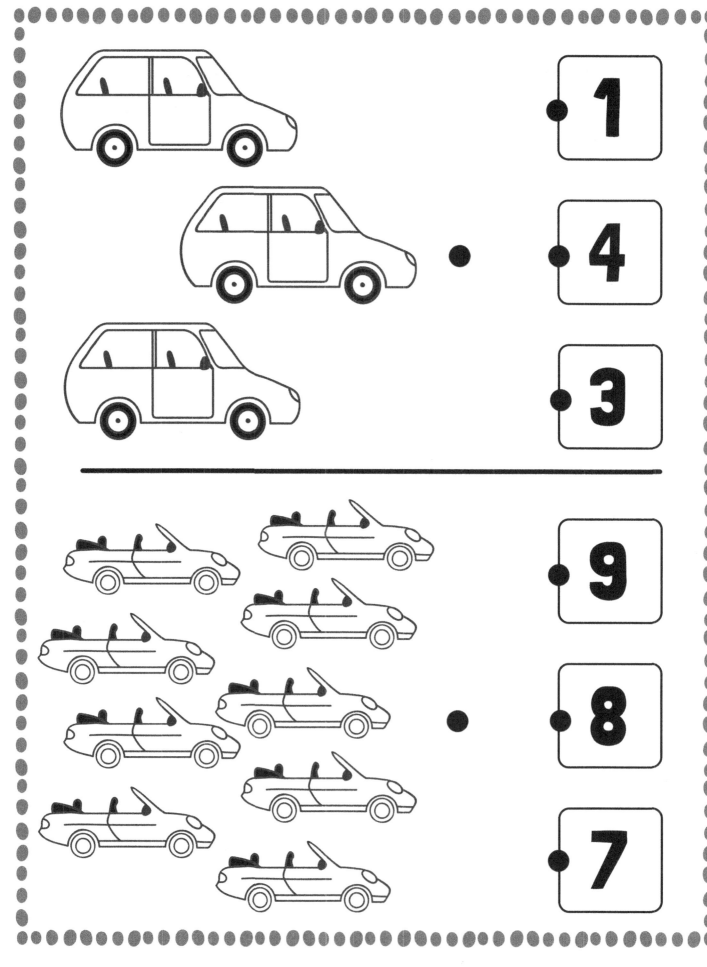

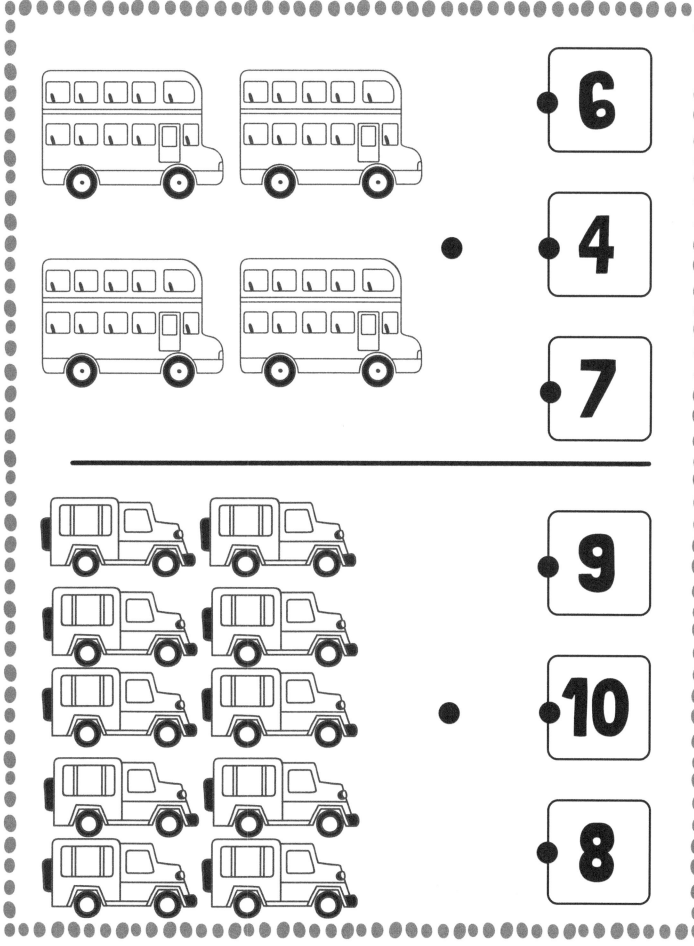

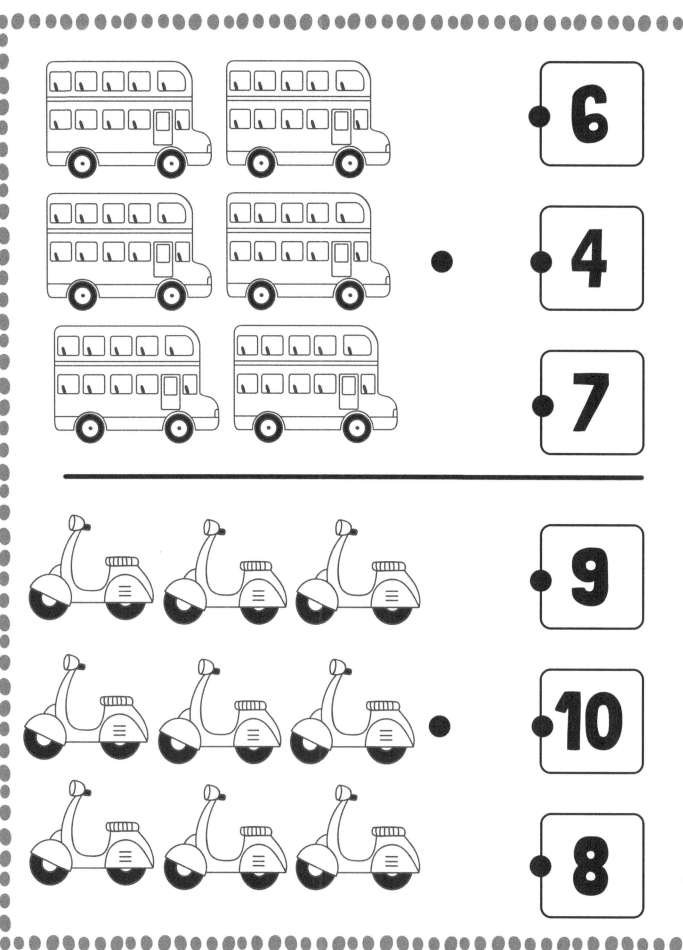

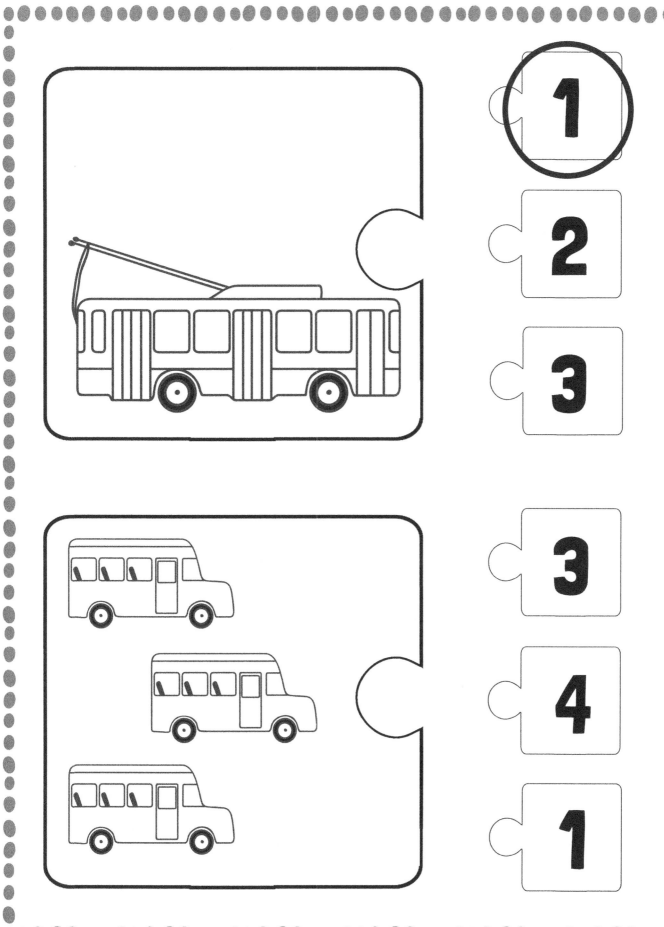

9

10

8

6

4

7

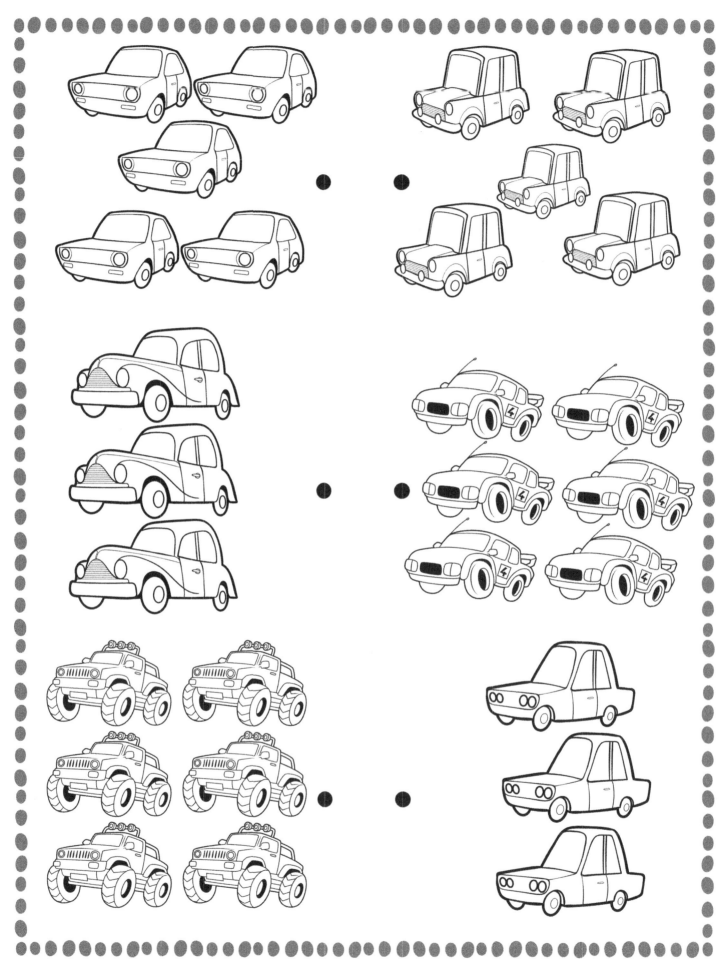

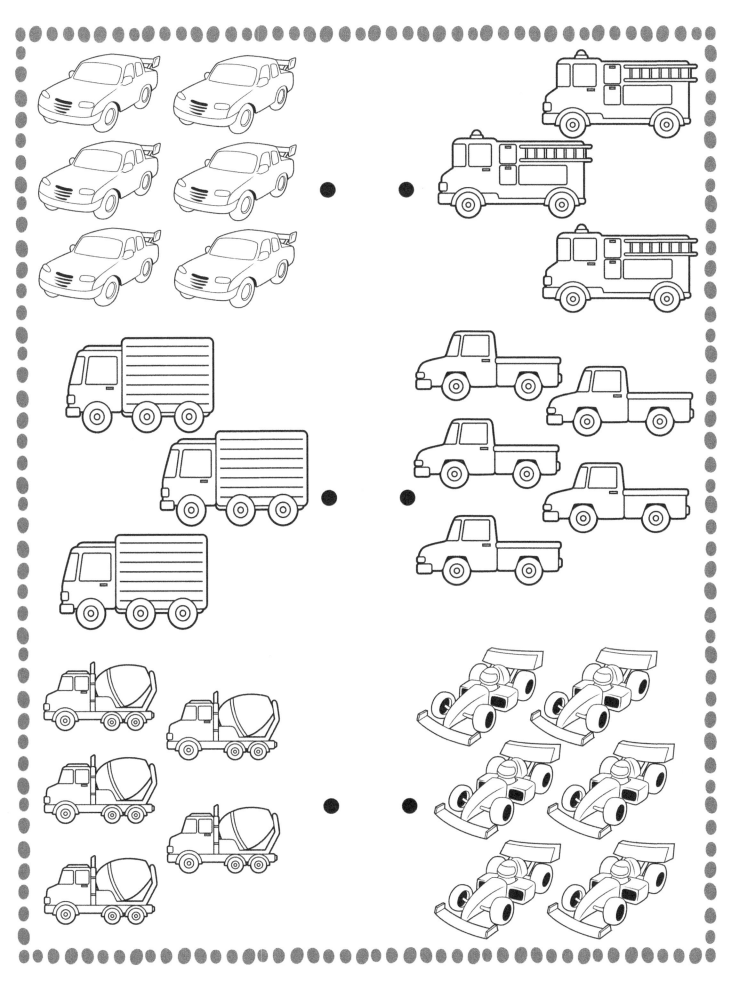

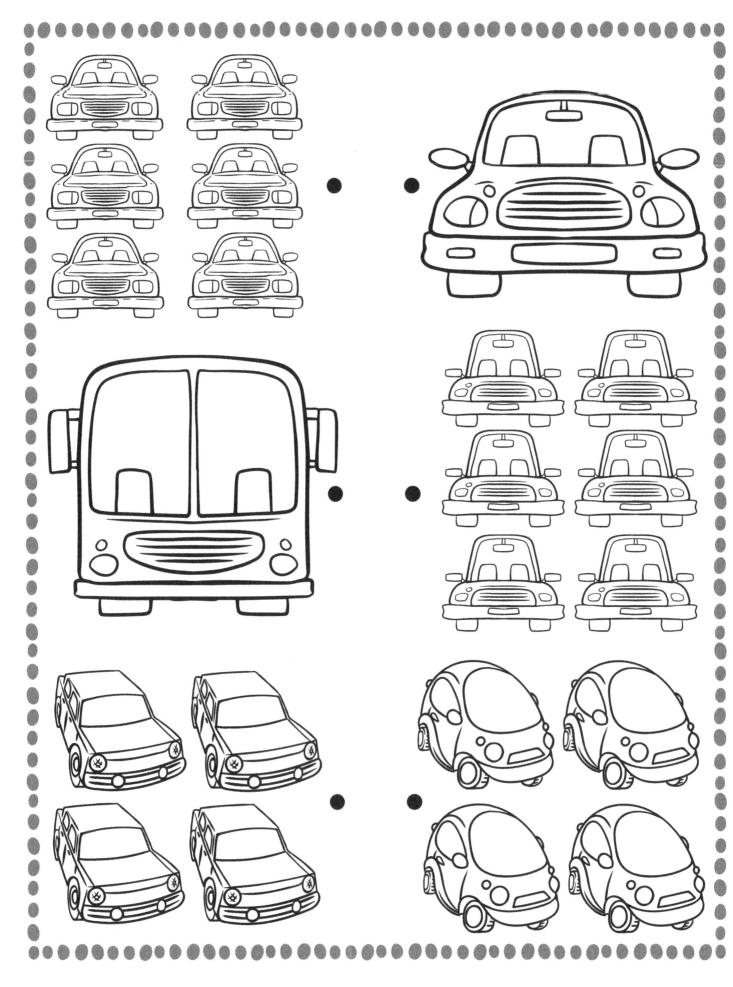

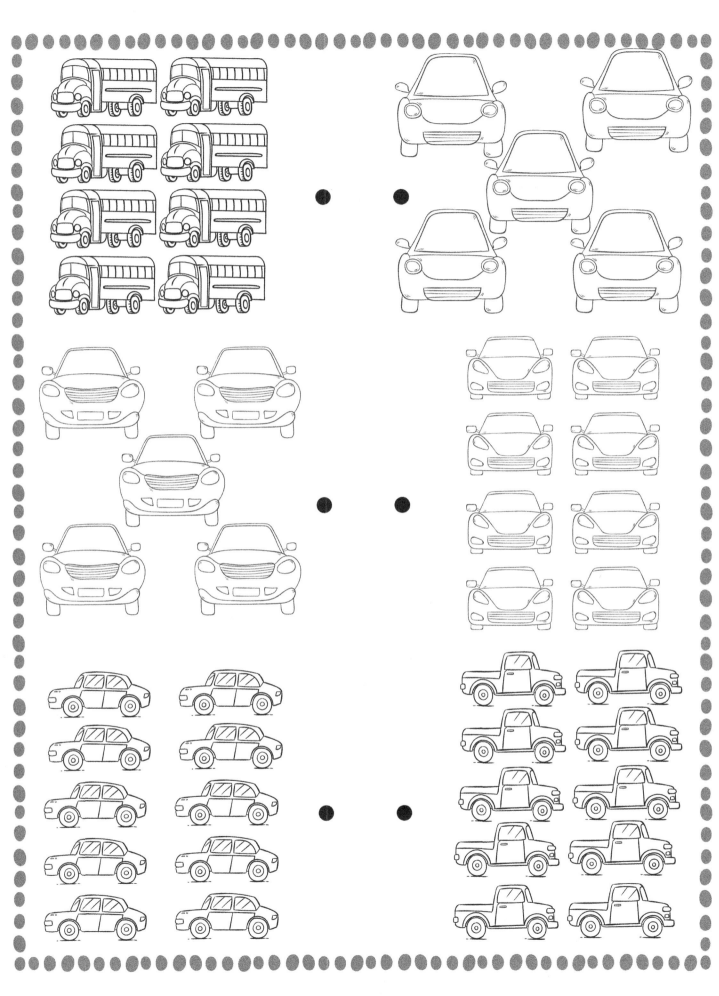

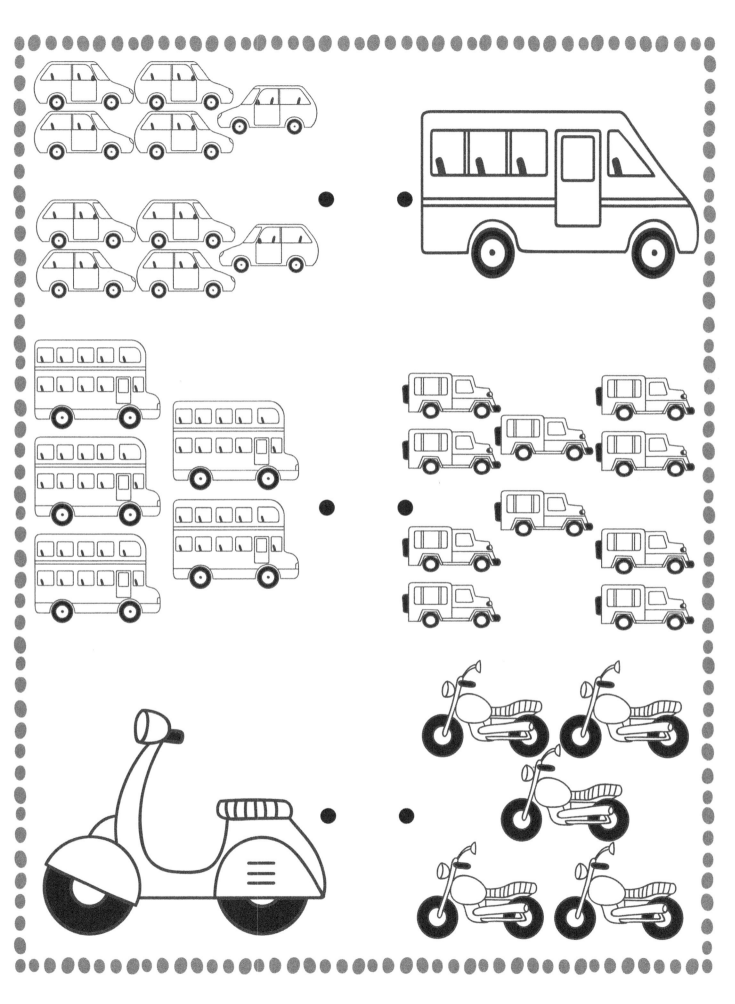

1
2
3

1
4
5

4
5
6

4
2
3

6
4
5

7
8
6

6
5
7

1
2
3

9
10
8

4

3

2

7

8

9

1

2

3

4
3
2

7
8
9

1
2
3

10
9
8

7
5
6

4
3
5

10

9

8

7

5

6

4

3

5

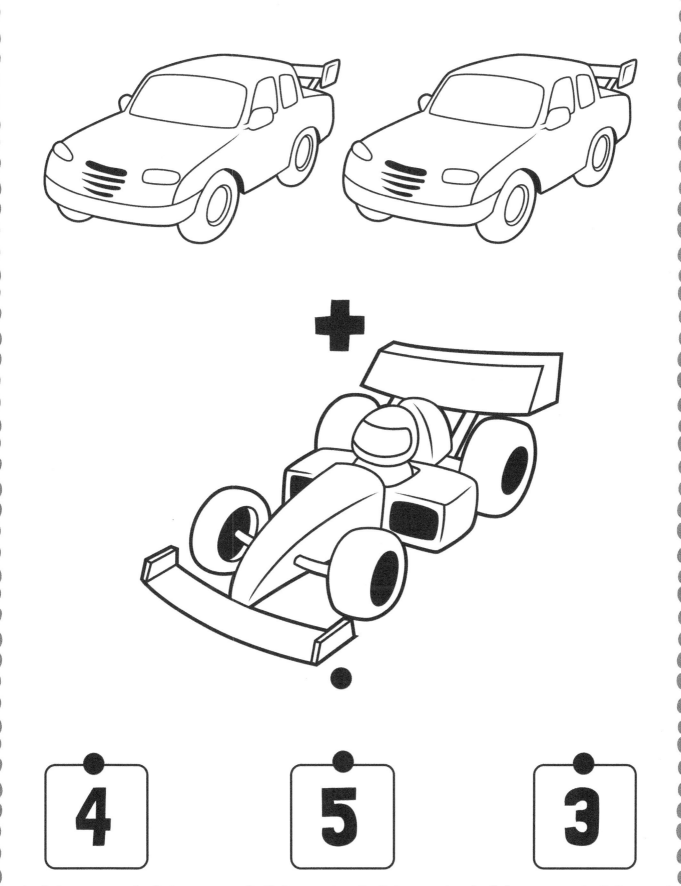

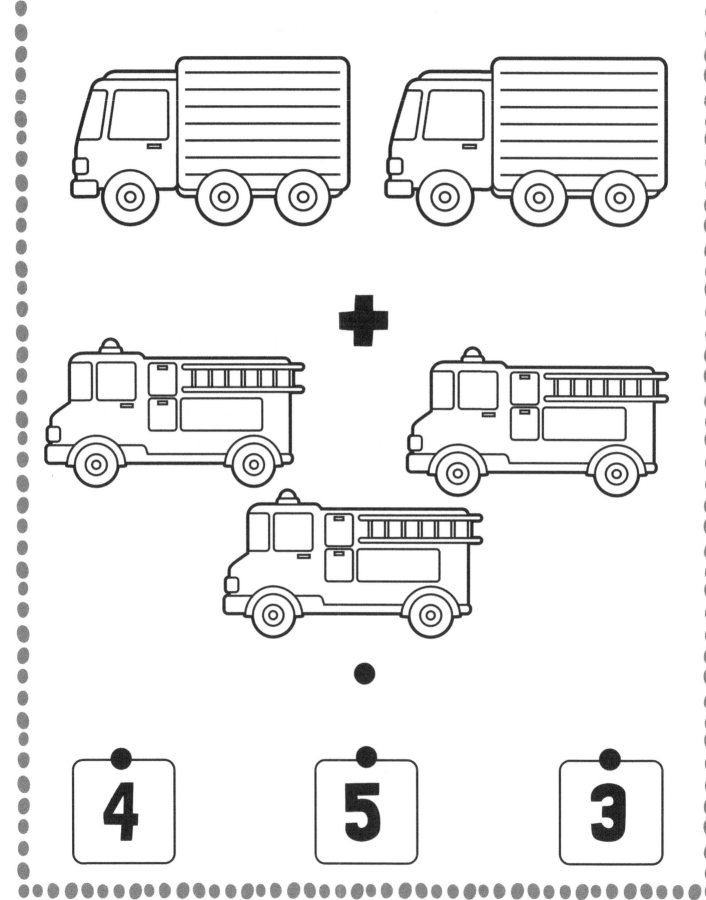

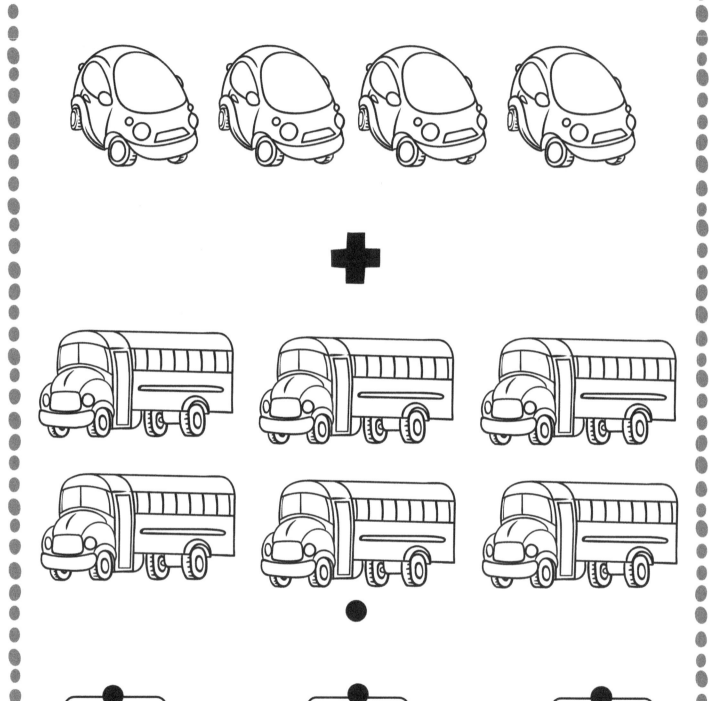

1 + 1 =

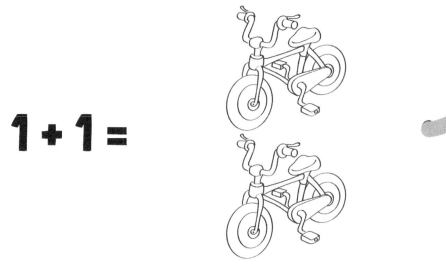

2

1

3

1 + 0 =

0

1

2

1 + 2 =

2

3

4

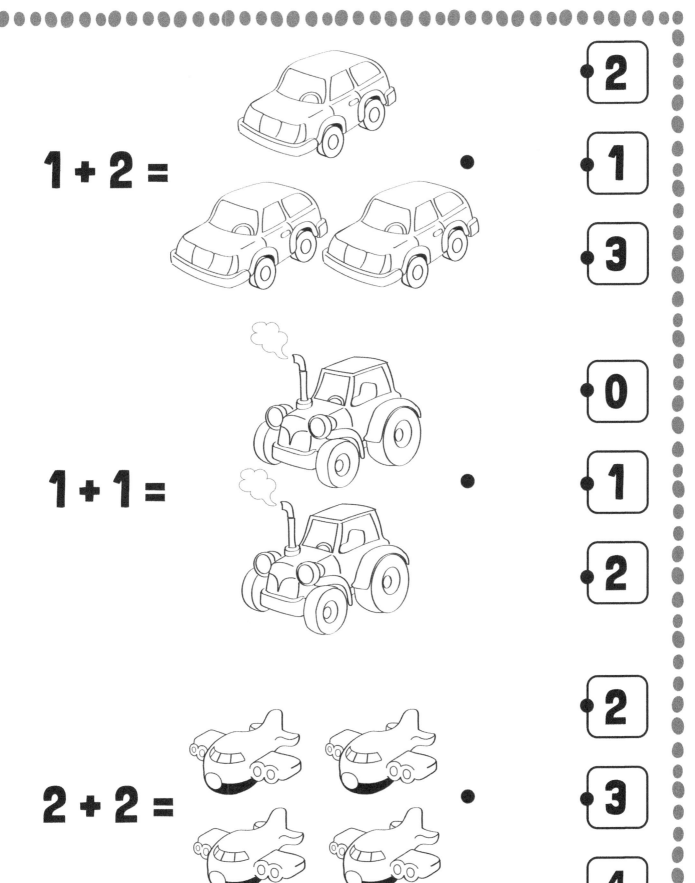

1 + 2 =

2

1

3

1 + 1 =

0

1

2

2 + 2 =

2

3

4

3 + 2 =    •

6

• **5**

• **3**

3 + 3 =  •

• **7**

• **8**

• **6**

2 + 3 =   •

• **3**

• **5**

• **4**

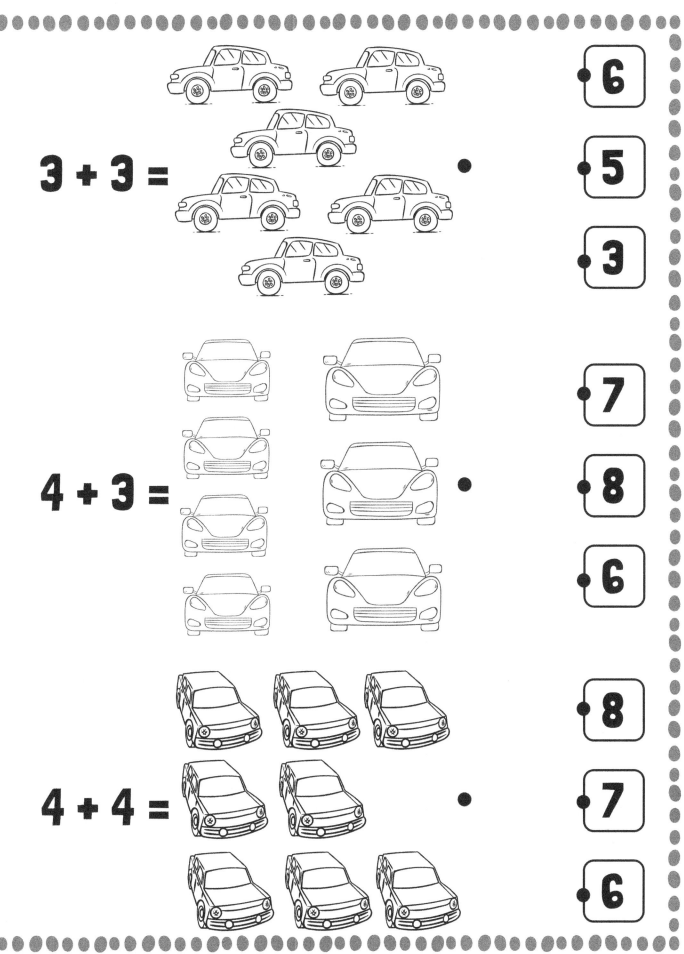

3 + 3 =

6
5
3

4 + 3 =

7
8
6

4 + 4 =

8
7
6

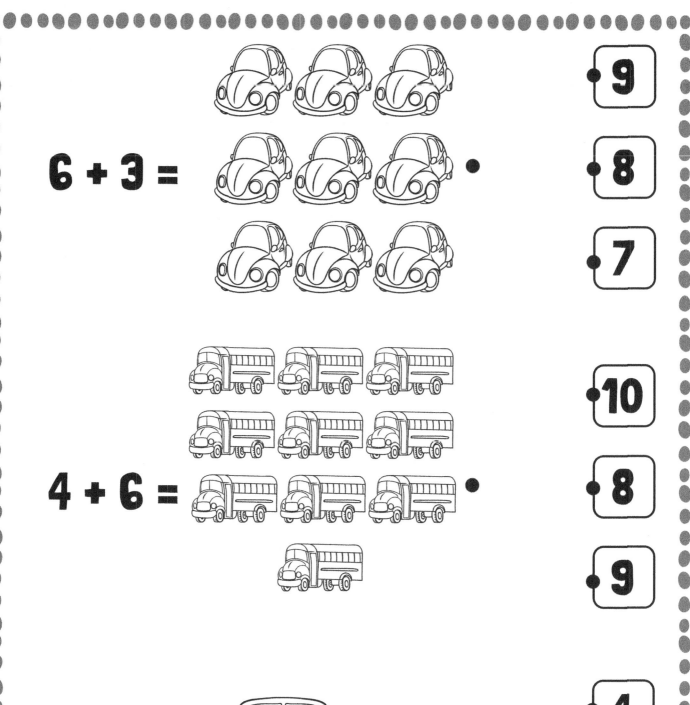

$6 + 3 =$ 9

              8

              7

$4 + 6 =$ 10

              8

              9

$2 + 0 =$ 4

              3

              2

Color Number 1

Color Number 2

Color Number 3

Color Number 4

Color Number 5

Color Number 6

Color Number 7

Color Number 8

Color Number 9

Made in the USA
Las Vegas, NV
06 May 2023